LEARNING ABOUT THE EARTH

Caves

by Emily K. Green

BELLWETHER MEDIA · MINNEAPOLIS, MN

Note to Librarians, Teachers, and Parents:

Blastoff! Readers are carefully developed by literacy experts and combine standards-based content with developmentally appropriate text.

Level 1 provides the most support through repetition of high-frequency words, light text, predictable sentence patterns, and strong visual support.

Level 2 offers early readers a bit more challenge through varied simple sentences, increased text load, and less repetition of high-frequency words.

Level 3 advances early-fluent readers toward fluency through increased text and concept load, less reliance on visuals, longer sentences, and more literary language.

Whichever book is right for your reader, Blastoff! Readers are the perfect books to build confidence and encourage a love of reading that will last a lifetime!

This edition first published in 2007 by Bellwether Media.

No part of this publication may be reproduced in whole or in part without written permission of the publisher. For information regarding permission, write to Bellwether Media Inc., Attention: Permissions Department, Post Office Box 1C, Minnetonka, MN 55345-9998.

Library of Congress Cataloging-in-Publication Data
Green, Emily K., 1966-
   Caves / by Emily K. Green.
      p. cm. — (Blastoff! readers) (Learning about the Earth)
Summary: "Simple text and supportive images introduce beginning readers to the physical characteristics and geographic locations of caves."
   Includes bibliographical references and index.
   ISBN-10: 1-60014-034-3 (hardcover : alk. paper)
   ISBN-13: 978-1-60014-034-1 (hardcover : alk. paper)
   1. Caves—Juvenile literature. I. Title. II. Series.

GB601.2.G74 2007
551.44'7—dc22   2006000568

Text copyright © 2007 by Bellwether Media.
Printed in the United States of America.

Table of Contents

Caves are rooms or tunnels
under the ground or in ice.

This is a sea cave. Ocean waves pound against cliffs and make sea caves.

Volcanoes make caves called **lava tubes**.

Hot **lava** flows from a volcano and then hardens like rock. When new lava flows it carves tubes in the hard lava.

This is an ice cave. Melting ice drips through cracks and carves ice caves.

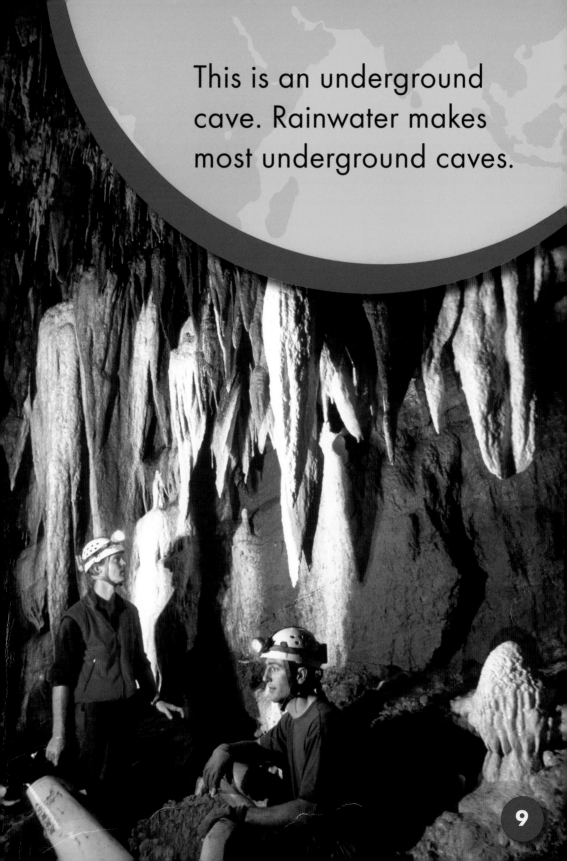

This is an underground cave. Rainwater makes most underground caves.

Rainwater flows through cracks in the ground. Water breaks down rock under the ground.

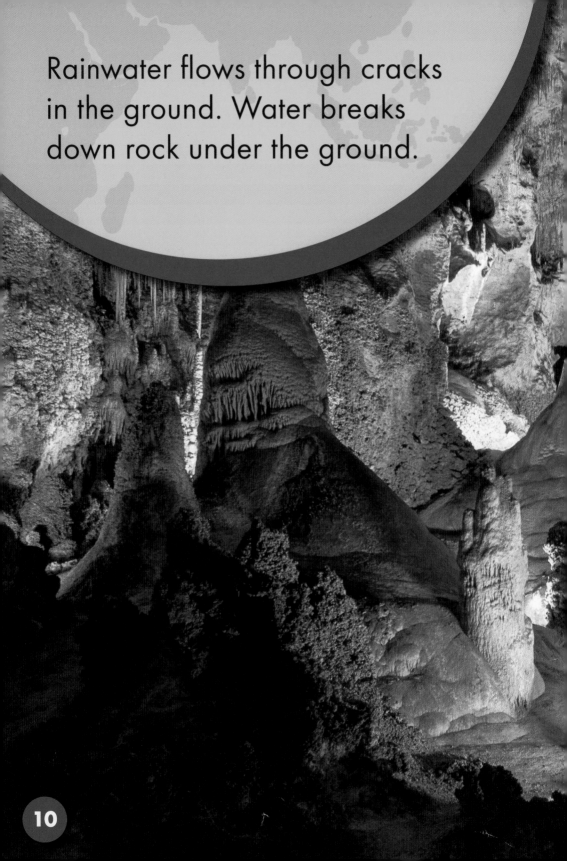

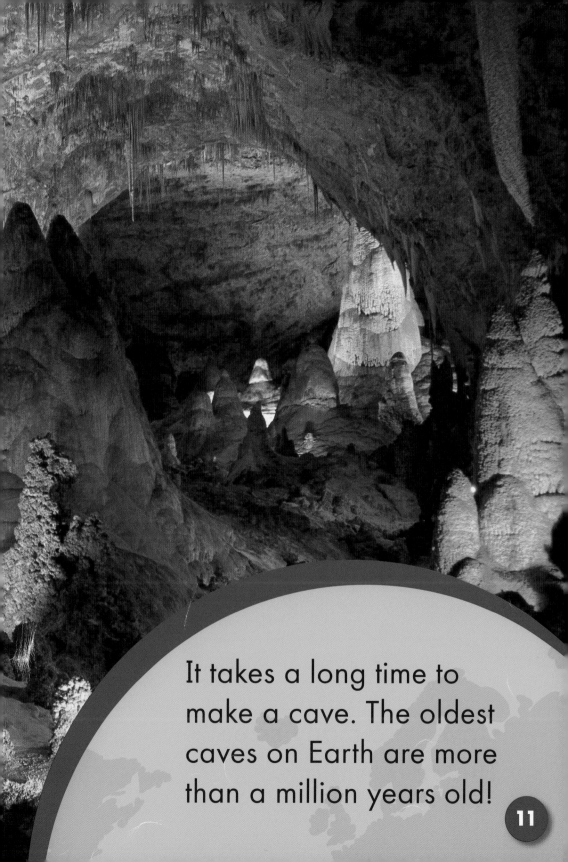

It takes a long time to make a cave. The oldest caves on Earth are more than a million years old!

Caves are many sizes.
This cave is big.

Some caves have many rooms. **Mammoth Cave** in Kentucky is one of the biggest caves on Earth.

Water flows through many caves. Sometimes water drips from the ceiling of a cave.

Water carries **minerals**. Some minerals harden and stick to the ceiling.

15

The minerals pile up into **cones** that hang from the ceiling. These are called **stalactites**.

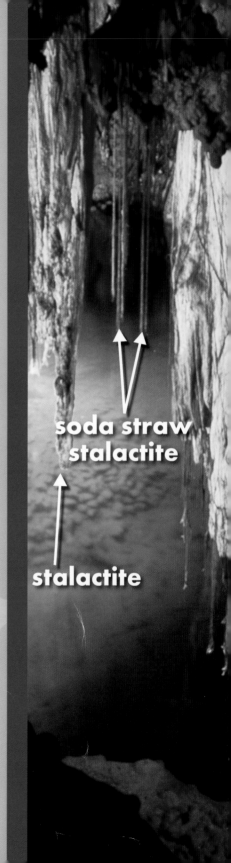

soda straw stalactite

stalactite

A soda straw stalactite is a **hollow** tube of minerals that hangs from the ceiling. Water drips through the tube.

stalagmite

Some water drips to the cave floor. The minerals harden and pile up on the floor. A cone of minerals that grows up from the floor is a **stalagmite**.

Stalactites and stalagmites form one drip at a time. After millions of drips, they might meet in the middle to form a **column**.

column

Caves are usually dark.
But sometimes people put
colorful lights in caves.

This cave holds an amazing world of shapes. What do you see?

Glossary

column—a pole that goes from the floor to the ceiling

cone—a triangle shape

hollow—empty

lava—hot, melted rock that flows out of a volcano; lava cools and hardens like rock.

lava tube—a cave made by a volcano

Mammoth Cave—a very big group of caves and tunnels in Kentucky, USA

minerals—a material found in nature; gold and iron are kinds of minerals.

stalactite—a cone of minerals hanging from the ceiling of a cave

stalagmite—a cone of minerals that grows up from the floor of a cave

To Learn More

AT THE LIBRARY

Davies, Nicola. *Bat Loves the Night*. Cambridge, Mass.: Candlewick, 2001.

Harrison, David L. *Caves: Mysteries Beneath Our Feet*. Honesdale, Penn.: Boyds Mills Press, 2001.

Siebert, Diane. *Cave*. New York: HarperCollins, 2000.

Taylor, Harriet Peck. *Secrets of the Stone*. New York: Farrar, Straus, and Giroux, 2002.

ON THE WEB

Learning more about caves is as easy as 1, 2, 3.

1. Go to www.factsurfer.com

2. Enter "caves" into search box.

3. Click the "Surf" button and you will see a list of related web sites.

With factsurfer.com, finding more information is just a click away.

Index

The photographs in this book are reproduced through the courtesy of: Tyler Stableford/Getty Images, front cover; David Hiser/Getty Images, p. 4; Kerrick James/Getty Images, p. 5; Bryan Busovicki, p. 6; G. Brad Lewis/Getty Images, p. 7; Fred Hirschmann/Getty Images, p. 8; Mark S. Cosslett/Getty Images, p. 9; Richard Nowitz/Getty Images, pp. 10-11; altrendo nature/Getty Images, pp. 12-13; China Tourism Press/Getty Images, pp. 14-15, 20-21; Demetrio Carrasco/Getty Images, pp. 16-17; Chad Ehlers/Getty Images, p. 18; altrendo travel/Getty Images, p. 19.